The Life Of A Lawyer: Daily Devotionals for Christian Legal Professionals

Delightful Devotionals

CONTENTS

Introduction

In the demanding realm of the law, where every decision carries profound consequences, maintaining a steadfast connection with God is not merely valuable; it is essential.

This 21-day devotional is crafted to be a constant companion on your legal journey, providing daily insights, scriptures, and reflections that resonate with the challenges and triumphs unique to your profession.

As a legal professional, the intricate tapestry of your career is woven with the threads of justice, mercy, wisdom, and resilience, and this devotional aims to explore how faith intertwines with each of these elements.

Each day invites you to a moment of reflection, offering inspiration and encouragement tailored to the rigors of your legal endeavors. It is a guide, not only through the complexities of the law but also through the complexities of the human experience within the legal profession.

As you navigate the intricate terrain of your career, may these daily reflections serve as a source of spiritual nourishment, providing clarity and purpose in your pursuit of justice.

Within these pages, you'll find a sanctuary for moments of pause, allowing your faith to anchor you in the midst of legal challenges.

This journey is an opportunity to delve into the profound connection between your professional life and your spiritual grounding, seeking a more purposeful and faith-filled approach to the practice of law.

May these 21 days become a transformative chapter in your ongoing story as a legal professional, enriching your perspective and fostering a deeper connection with your calling.

Day 1: Embracing Righteousness in Legal Practice

Verse of the Day:

Proverbs 21:3 - "To do what is right and just is more acceptable to the Lord than sacrifice."

Reflection:

As legal practitioners, our pursuit of justice is intertwined with a higher calling – the call to do what is right and just. Proverbs 21:3 encourages us to prioritize righteousness over external offerings, emphasizing the profound impact of ethical conduct and integrity in our legal endeavors.

In the simplicity of living righteously, we find a path that not only aligns with the divine but also resonates with the core of our professional identity.

Today, let us embrace the simplicity of doing what is right and just. In our legal actions, no matter how intricate the case or challenging the circumstances, righteousness becomes our guide.

As we navigate the complexities of legal practice, may the pursuit of justice be woven seamlessly with the fabric of righteousness, bringing honor to our calling as lawyers and reflecting the values of our faith.

Journal:

1. How can I infuse righteousness into the daily decisions and actions of my legal practice?

2. Reflect on a moment when prioritizing justice over personal gain had a positive impact.

3. In what ways can I seek divine guidance to ensure that my legal actions align with God's standards of righteousness?

Prayer:

Heavenly Father, guide us in our legal pursuits, reminding us that in simplicity, righteousness prevails. Grant us wisdom to navigate complexities with integrity, and may our commitment to justice be a reflection of Your divine standards. Amen.

Day 2: Nurturing Faithful Stewardship

Verse of the Day:

Joshua 1:9 - "Have I not commanded you? Be strong and courageous. Do not be afraid; do not be discouraged, for the Lord your God will be with you wherever you go."

Reflection:

In the tapestry of legal practice, our skills are not merely tools for professional success but divine gifts entrusted to us. Matthew 25:21 reminds us that faithful stewardship of these talents brings joy to the Master.

Today, let us embrace the responsibility of being stewards of our legal abilities, recognizing the impact our faithful management can have on the lives of others.

As legal stewards, we hold the privilege of influencing justice and shaping the legal landscape.

By faithfully managing our talents, we not only fulfill our professional duties but also contribute to a just and compassionate legal system.

In each legal action, let us be mindful of the divine call to stewardship, understanding that our actions echo beyond the courtroom, resonating with the joy of the One who entrusted us.

Journal:

1. How can I consciously integrate faithful stewardship into my daily legal practice?

2. Reflect on a situation where you felt you faithfully utilized your legal talents. What impact did it have?

3. In what ways can I continually grow and develop my legal skills as a faithful steward?

Prayer:

Lord, as stewards of legal talents, we seek Your guidance. Grant us wisdom to manage our skills faithfully, using them for the betterment of society and the pursuit of justice. May our actions bring joy to You, our Master, as we navigate the complexities of legal service. Amen.

Day 3: Infusing Compassion into Legal Advocacy

Verse of the Day:

Colossians 3:12 - "Therefore, as God's chosen people, holy and dearly loved, clothe yourselves with compassion, kindness, humility, gentleness, and patience."

Reflection:

In the pursuit of justice, Colossians 3:12 calls us to clothe ourselves with compassion, recognizing it as an essential garment for those chosen by God. Today, let's delve into the significance of practicing compassion in our legal advocacy.

As legal practitioners, our actions can extend beyond the courtroom, leaving a lasting impact on those we serve. Compassion is not just a virtue; it's a transformative force in legal advocacy.

When we approach our clients and cases with kindness, humility, and patience, we emulate the divine compassion bestowed upon us.

Today, let's intentionally infuse compassion into our legal practice, fostering a more empathetic and just legal system.

Journal:

1. How can I consciously exhibit compassion in my interactions with clients, colleagues, and all those involved in legal proceedings?

2. Recall a moment when practicing compassion positively influenced a legal outcome. How did it shape the experience for all parties involved?

3. In what ways can I nurture a compassionate mindset in the often-demanding field of legal advocacy?

Prayer:

Gracious God, as we advocate for justice, may our hearts be filled with Your compassionate spirit. Help us to embody kindness, humility, and patience in our legal endeavors, creating a space where justice and empathy intersect. Amen.

Day 4: Seeking Divine Guidance in Legal Decision-Making

Verse of the Day:

James 1:5 - "If any of you lacks wisdom, you should ask God, who gives generously to all without finding fault, and it will be given to you."

Reflection:

In the intricate web of legal decisions, James 1:5 provides a guiding light – an invitation to seek divine wisdom. Today, let us explore the profound impact of aligning our legal decision-making with the wisdom generously granted by God.

As legal practitioners, acknowledging our need for divine guidance can elevate our discernment and foster just outcomes.

Legal decisions carry weight, and in the quest for justice, seeking divine wisdom becomes our compass. God's generosity in providing wisdom is not bound by fault or hesitation.

Let us, therefore, approach our legal decision-making with a humble heart, seeking the wisdom that transcends human understanding.

Journal:

1. How can I intentionally invite divine guidance into my legal decision-making process?

2. Reflect on a situation where seeking God's wisdom influenced a legal outcome. What lessons did you learn?

3. In what ways can I cultivate a mindset of humility and openness to divine guidance in my legal practice?

Prayer:

Heavenly Father, grant us the wisdom to navigate the complexities of legal decision-making. May our hearts be open to Your guidance, seeking wisdom that goes beyond human understanding. Guide our minds and actions as we make decisions that impact the lives of others. Amen.

Day 5: Balancing Justice and Mercy in Legal Actions

Verse of the Day:

"He has shown you, O mortal, what is good. And what does the Lord require of you? To act justly and to love mercy and to walk humbly with your God."

Reflection:

In the delicate dance of legal actions, Micah 6:8 unfolds a divine blueprint – a call to balance justice and mercy.

Today, let us delve into the profound wisdom of harmonizing these virtues in our legal practice. As agents of justice, recognizing the intertwined nature of justice and mercy enriches the impact of our legal actions.

Justice and mercy are not opposing forces but complementary virtues. Micah's wisdom encourages us to act justly while embracing the compassion of mercy.

In legal actions, let's strive for this delicate balance, understanding that true justice is seasoned with mercy and humility.

Journal:

1. How do I currently balance justice and mercy in my legal actions?

2. Recall a situation where balancing justice and mercy led to a more equitable outcome. What principles guided your approach?

3. In what ways can I deepen my understanding of justice and mercy in the context of legal practice?

Prayer:

Merciful God, as we navigate the complexities of legal actions, guide us in balancing justice and mercy. May our decisions reflect Your divine wisdom, acting justly while embracing the transformative power of mercy. Help us to walk humbly in Your grace. Amen.

Day 6: Guidance in the Chaos

Verse of the Day:

Proverbs 11:3 - "The integrity of the upright guides them, but the unfaithful are destroyed by their duplicity."

Reflection:

In the landscape of legal practice, Proverbs 11:3 unveils the cornerstone – integrity. Today, let us explore the profound significance of integrity as the bedrock of our legal endeavors.

As stewards of justice, embracing unwavering integrity guides our actions and upholds the principles of righteousness.

Integrity is the compass that steers us through the complexities of legal practice. Proverbs paints a vivid picture of the upright guided by integrity and warns of the destruction that follows duplicity.

Let our commitment to integrity shine as a beacon, fostering trust and righteousness in our legal interactions.

Journal:

1. How does integrity manifest in my daily legal practice, and where can I enhance its presence?

2. Recall a challenging situation where upholding integrity was paramount. What were the outcomes, and what lessons were learned?

3. In what ways can I influence a culture of integrity within the legal community?

Prayer:

Gracious Lord, instill in us the unwavering commitment to integrity in our legal practice. May our actions be guided by honesty and righteousness, reflecting the uprightness described in Proverbs. Guard us against duplicity and lead us in the path of unwavering integrity. Amen.

Day 7: Finding Strength in Faith During Legal Challenges

Verse of the Day:

Romans 8:28 - "And we know that in all things God works for the good of those who love him, who have been called according to his purpose."

Reflection:

Amidst the legal challenges that may seem insurmountable, Romans 8:28 becomes a source of strength and hope.

Today, let us delve into the assurance that, even in the face of legal complexities, our faith can be an anchor, and God works all things for the good of those who love Him.

In the midst of legal challenges, our faith becomes a wellspring of strength. Romans 8:28 reassures us that God orchestrates events for our good.

As legal practitioners, let us draw strength from this promise, trusting that our challenges are not in vain but part of a greater purpose.

Journal:

1. How has my faith influenced my approach to legal challenges in the past?

2. Recall a situation where, in hindsight, you recognized God's work for good in a legal matter. How did it shape your perspective?

3. In what ways can I strengthen my faith to navigate future legal challenges with resilience and hope?

Prayer:

Heavenly Father, grant us strength in the face of legal challenges. May our faith be unwavering, trusting that You work all things for our good. Guide us in aligning our purpose with Yours, finding hope and resilience in the assurance of Your divine plan. Amen.

Day 8: Patience in Legal Processes: Trusting God's Timing

Verse of the Day:

Proverbs 14:29 - "Whoever is patient has great understanding, but one who is quick-tempered displays folly."

Reflection:

In the labyrinth of legal processes, Proverbs 14:29 shines as a guiding light, emphasizing the virtue of patience. Today, let us explore the profound wisdom of patiently navigating legal timelines, trusting in God's perfect timing.

Patience is a cornerstone in the legal journey. Proverbs extols the understanding that comes with patience, contrasting it with the folly of impatience.

In legal processes, cultivating patience allows for discernment and a more measured approach.

Journal:

1. How has impatience hindered or influenced my legal processes in the past?

2. Reflect on a situation where patience yielded positive outcomes in a legal matter. What lessons were learned?

3. In what ways can I foster patience in my daily legal practice, both personally and professionally?

Prayer:

Gracious God, in the intricate dance of legal processes, grant us the virtue of patience. May we trust Your timing, knowing that patience leads to understanding. Guard us against quick-tempered folly and guide us in navigating legal timelines with wisdom. Amen.

Day 9: Building Bridges and Unity in Legal Relationships

Verse of the day:

Ephesians 4:3 - "Make every effort to keep the unity of the Spirit through the bond of peace."

Reflection:

In the realm of legal relationships, Ephesians 4:3 invites us to actively pursue unity and peace.

Today, let us explore the significance of building bridges and fostering unity in the diverse landscape of legal interactions.

Unity is a powerful force that brings strength to legal relationships. Ephesians encourages us to make every effort to keep the unity of the Spirit, emphasizing the bond of peace.

In legal practice, cultivating unity promotes collaboration and harmony.

Journal:

1. How do I currently contribute to building unity in my legal relationships, both within and outside my firm or practice?

2. Recall a challenging legal interaction where unity was crucial. How did the pursuit of unity impact the outcome?

3. In what ways can I proactively foster a spirit of unity and peace in the legal community?

Prayer:

Heavenly Father, guide us in building bridges and promoting unity in our legal relationships. May the Spirit of unity and peace be a guiding force in our interactions. Grant us wisdom to navigate diversity, fostering collaboration and understanding in the legal landscape. Amen.

Day 10: Wisdom in Legal Strategy: Seeking God's Counsel

Verse of the Day:

James 1:5 - "If any of you lacks wisdom, you should ask God, who gives generously to all without finding fault, and it will be given to you."

Reflection:

In the intricate realm of legal strategy, James 1:5 serves as a beacon, reminding us to seek God's counsel for wisdom.

Today, let us explore the profound impact of infusing our legal decisions with divine wisdom. Wisdom is a precious asset in legal strategy.

James encourages us to seek God, the Giver of wisdom. In legal decisions, relying on divine counsel ensures a foundation built on insight, discernment, and a broader perspective.

Journal:

1. How has seeking God's counsel impacted my legal strategies in the past?

2. Reflect on a situation where divine wisdom guided a legal decision. What were the outcomes?

3. In what areas of my legal practice can I more intentionally seek God's counsel for wisdom?

Prayer:

Lord of Wisdom, as we navigate the complexities of legal strategy, grant us the discernment that comes from seeking Your counsel. May divine wisdom guide our decisions, ensuring that we approach legal challenges with insight and understanding. In Your name, we pray. Amen.

Day 11: Humility in Legal Leadership

Verse of the Day:

Philippians 2:3-4 - "Do nothing out of selfish ambition or vain conceit. Rather, in humility value others above yourselves, not looking to your own interests but each of you to the interests of the others."

Reflection:

In the arena of legal leadership, Philippians 2:3-4 calls us to embrace humility and prioritize the interests of others. Today, let us explore the transformative power of humility in legal leadership.

Humility is the cornerstone of effective leadership. Philippians reminds us to prioritize others over ourselves, fostering a culture of collaboration and shared success.

In legal leadership, humility invites respect, trust, and a harmonious work environment.

Journal:

1. How does humility contribute to effective legal leadership?

2. Recall a situation where humility played a crucial role in resolving a legal challenge. What lessons were learned?

3. In what ways can I cultivate humility in my legal leadership style, fostering a collaborative and supportive team?

Prayer:

Gracious God, instill in us the virtue of humility as we lead in the legal realm. May we value others above ourselves and be guided by the interests of those we lead. Grant us the wisdom to lead with grace and humility. Amen.

Day 12: Resilience in the Face of Legal Criticism

Verse of the Day:

Psalm 31:24 - "Be strong and take heart, all you who hope in the LORD.

Reflection:

In the legal landscape, facing criticism is inevitable. Psalm 31:24 encourages us to be strong and take heart, especially in the face of legal critique. Today, let us explore the resilience that comes from anchoring our hope in the Lord.

Resilience is a vital quality in navigating legal criticism. Psalm 31:24 reassures us that our strength and courage can be rooted in the hope we have in the Lord.

Embracing resilience enables us to learn and grow from criticism, turning challenges into opportunities for improvement.

Journal:

1. How do I typically respond to legal criticism, and how can I cultivate resilience in such situations?

2. Recall a challenging moment where resilience played a crucial role in overcoming legal critique. What insights did you gain?

3. In what ways can I anchor my hope in the Lord to foster resilience in the face of legal challenges?

Prayer:

Heavenly Father, grant us resilience in the face of legal criticism. May our hope in You be a source of strength, enabling us to navigate challenges with courage and grace. Teach us to learn and grow from critique, becoming better advocates for justice. Amen.

Day 13: Cultivating Justice, Mercy, and Humility

Verse of the Day:

Micah 6:8 - "He has shown you, O mortal, what is good. And what does the Lord require of you? To act justly and to love mercy and to walk humbly with your God."

Reflection:

Micah 6:8 beautifully encapsulates the divine call to cultivate justice, mercy, and humility in our legal practice.

Today, let us explore the transformative impact of embodying these virtues. In the pursuit of justice, we are called to intertwine it with mercy and humility.

Micah's verse reminds us that a harmonious balance of justice and mercy, coupled with a humble demeanor, reflects the divine standard for our legal endeavors.

Journal

1.   How can I actively integrate justice, mercy, and humility into my legal practice?

2.   Reflect on a case where the pursuit of justice was balanced with mercy. What were the outcomes?

3.   In what ways can I cultivate a humble attitude in the midst of legal responsibilities and challenges?

Prayer:

Gracious God, guide us as we seek to cultivate justice, mercy, and humility in our legal practice. May our actions reflect Your divine standards, and may our pursuit of justice be infused with compassion and humility. In Your name, we pray. Amen.

Day 14: Restoring Hope in Legal Communities

Verse of the Day:

Matthew 5:16 - "In the same way, let your light shine before others, that they may see your good deeds and glorify your Father in heaven."

Reflection:

Matthew 5:16 inspires us to restore hope in legal communities by letting our light shine through good deeds.

Today, let us explore the profound impact of bringing hope to the forefront of our legal endeavors. Restoring hope in legal communities is a transformative act.

Matthew 5:16 encourages us to be beacons of light, showcasing compassion and justice through our actions. By doing so, we contribute to the well-being and upliftment of the legal community.

Journal:

1. How can I actively contribute to restoring hope within the legal community?

2. Reflect on a time when a small act positively influenced the legal community's morale. What can be learned from that experience?

3. In what ways can I let my light shine through good deeds in the legal realm?

Prayer:

Heavenly Father, empower us to be agents of hope in legal communities. May our actions glorify You, and may our efforts contribute to a sense of positivity, justice, and unity within the legal profession. Guide us as we seek to make a positive impact. Amen.

Day 15: Trusting God's Guidance in Legal Decisions

Verse of the Day:

Proverbs 3:5-6 - "Trust in the LORD with all your heart and lean not on your own understanding; in all your ways submit to him, and he will make your paths straight."

Reflection:

Proverbs 3:5-6 provides a foundational truth for legal professionals – trusting God's guidance in our decisions.

Today, let's delve into the profound wisdom of relying on God's direction in our legal journey. In the complex landscape of legal decisions, trust becomes our anchor.

Proverbs teaches us that entrusting our hearts to the Lord and submitting our ways to Him lead to a straightened path. Trusting God's guidance brings clarity and purpose to our legal decisions.

Journal:

1. How intentional am I about seeking God's guidance in my legal decisions?

2. Reflect on a decision where relying on God's guidance made a significant difference. What insights did you gain?

3. In what ways can I deepen my trust in God's guidance throughout my legal practice?

Prayer:

Lord, grant us the wisdom to trust Your guidance in every legal decision. Help us lean not on our understanding but rely on Your infinite wisdom. May our hearts be attuned to Your leading, making our paths straight. In Your name, we pray. Amen.

Day 16: Sacrificial Love in Legal Service

Verse of the Day:

John 15:13 - "Greater love has no one than this: to lay down one's life for one's friends."

Reflection:

John 15:13 emphasizes sacrificial love, a profound concept that extends to the heart of legal service. Let's explore the transformative power of sacrificial love in our legal endeavors.

Sacrificial love involves selflessness and putting others' needs above our own. In legal service, embodying this love can lead to profound impacts on clients, colleagues, and the community.

John 15:13 sets a high standard, inspiring us to consider the well-being of others above all.

Journal:

1. How can I demonstrate sacrificial love in my legal interactions and service?

2. Reflect on a time when sacrificial love made a significant impact on a legal situation. What lessons can be drawn?

3. In what ways can sacrificial love transform the dynamics of legal relationships and advocacy?

Prayer:

Gracious God, teach us the depth of sacrificial love in our legal service. May our actions reflect the selfless love demonstrated by Christ. Help us lay down our own interests for the well-being of others, fostering a culture of love in the legal realm. Amen.

Day 17: Building Peaceful Connections in Legal Practice

Verse of the Day:

Romans 12:18 - "If it is possible, as far as it depends on you, live at peace with everyone."

Reflection:

Romans 12:18 calls us to actively pursue peace in our interactions, a principle profoundly relevant to legal practice.

Let's explore the transformative impact of building peaceful connections in our legal journey. The legal profession often involves navigating conflicts, but Romans 12:18 encourages us to be peacemakers.

Building peaceful connections contributes to a harmonious legal environment, fostering understanding and resolution.

Journal:

1. How can I actively contribute to building peace in legal relationships?

2. Reflect on a situation where promoting peace had a positive impact on legal outcomes. What strategies were effective?

3. In what ways can I balance zealous advocacy with a commitment to peace in legal practice?

Prayer:

Heavenly Father, guide us in building peaceful connections in our legal interactions. Grant us the wisdom to pursue peace, even in challenging situations. May our legal practice be marked by harmony, understanding, and a commitment to resolution. In Your name, we pray. Amen.

Day 18: Finding Joy and Purpose in Legal Service

Verse of the Day:

Galatians 5:22-23 - "But the fruit of the Spirit is love, joy, peace, forbearance, kindness, goodness, faithfulness, gentleness, and self-control. Against such things, there is no law."

Reflection:

Galatians 5:22-23 highlights the fruits of the Spirit, including joy. Let's explore how finding joy and purpose in legal service can transform our approach to the practice of law.

In the pursuit of justice, joy can be a powerful force. Galatians reminds us that joy is a fruit of the Spirit, suggesting that it is an integral part of our spiritual journey.

Finding joy in legal service not only benefits us personally but also positively influences those we serve.

Journal:

1. What brings joy and purpose to my legal practice?

2. Reflect on a case or situation where joy played a role in overcoming challenges. How did it impact the outcome?

3. In what ways can I cultivate joy in the midst of the demands and pressures of legal service?

Prayer:

Heavenly Father, infuse our legal service with the joy that comes from Your Spirit. Help us find purpose in promoting justice and upholding righteousness. May our work be marked by the joy that emanates from a deep connection with You. Amen.

Day 19: Embracing Diversity in Legal Advocacy

Verse of the Day:

Revelation 7:9 - "After this I looked, and there before me was a great multitude that no one could count, from every nation, tribe, people, and language, standing before the throne and before the Lamb."

Reflection:

Revelation 7:9 paints a vivid picture of diversity, reminding us of the richness found in different backgrounds.

Let's explore the significance of embracing diversity in our legal advocacy.

Diversity is a source of strength. In the legal field, embracing diverse perspectives enhances our ability to navigate complex issues, fostering innovation and understanding. John's vision in Revelation encourages us to appreciate the beauty of diversity in legal advocacy.

Journal:

1. How does embracing diversity contribute to effective legal advocacy?

2. Reflect on a case where diverse perspectives played a crucial role. What lessons did you learn?

3. In what ways can I actively promote inclusivity and diversity in my legal work?

Prayer:

Lord, help us embrace diversity in our legal advocacy. Open our hearts to appreciate the richness that different perspectives bring. May our legal practices reflect the inclusivity found in Your diverse creation. Amen.

Day 20: Gratitude in Legal Service

Verse of the Day:

1 Thessalonians 5:18 - "Give thanks in all circumstances; for this is God's will for you in Christ Jesus."

Reflection:

The practice of gratitude transforms our perspective and approach to legal service. Let's explore the role of gratitude in our professional lives.

Gratitude is a powerful attitude that can shape our experiences in legal service.

1 Thessalonians 5:18 encourages us to give thanks in all circumstances, reminding us that a grateful heart brings about positive change.

Journal:

1. What are some aspects of my legal practice for which I am grateful?

2. How does expressing gratitude impact my interactions with colleagues, clients, and the legal community?

3. In challenging situations, how can I cultivate gratitude to navigate difficulties with a positive mindset?

Prayer:

Heavenly Father, instill in us a heart of gratitude as we engage in legal service. Help us recognize and appreciate the opportunities, challenges, and relationships that shape our professional journey. May our work be a reflection of thankfulness and Your enduring grace. Amen.

Day 21: A Legacy of Faithfulness in Legal Careers

Verse of the Day:

2 Timothy 4:7-8 - "I have fought the good fight, I have finished the race, I have kept the faith. Now there is in store for me the crown of righteousness, which the Lord, the righteous Judge, will award to me on that day—and not only to me, but also to all who have longed for his appearing."

Reflection:

As we conclude this devotional journey for legal professionals, let's reflect on leaving a legacy of faithfulness in our legal careers.

2 Timothy 4:7-8 inspires us to view our legal careers as a race of faithfulness. Each case, each interaction, contributes to a legacy.

May our legal endeavors be marked by the endurance that leads to a crown of righteousness.

Journal:

1. What does a legacy of faithfulness mean to me in the context of my legal career?

2. Reflect on a moment when faithfulness played a significant role in a legal decision or action.

3. How can I actively contribute to a legacy of faithfulness for those who will follow in my legal footsteps?

Prayer:

Gracious God, as we conclude this devotional journey, we seek Your guidance to leave a legacy of faithfulness in our legal careers. Grant us the strength to fight the good fight, finish the race, and keep the faith. May our professional journeys be a testament to Your enduring grace. In Your name, we pray. Amen.

Conclusion

As we conclude this 21-day journey, we stand at the intersection of faith and legal practice, recognizing the profound impact our beliefs can have on the pursuit of justice. Each day has been a step towards a deeper understanding of the divine calling embedded in our legal careers.

Remember, your work as legal professionals is not merely a vocation; it is a unique opportunity to manifest justice, compassion, and integrity in a world that often yearns for these virtues. The legal field is not devoid of challenges, but our faith equips us to face them with resilience, wisdom, and an unwavering commitment to truth.

As you navigate the complexities of your legal journey, may the lessons from this devotional resonate in your hearts, guiding your decisions and actions. May you carry the torch of faithfulness, leaving a legacy that extends beyond courtrooms and documents – a legacy that embodies the principles of justice, mercy, and unwavering faith.

May your legal careers be marked not only by professional success but by a profound sense of purpose rooted in faith.

Embrace each day with the knowledge that your advocacy, guided by faith, contributes to a more just and compassionate world.

In faith and gratitude,

Delightful Devotionals